BOTTLENOSE DOLPHINS

ELIZABETH THOMAS

Published in the United States of America by Cherry Lake Publishing
Ann Arbor, Michigan
www.cherrylakepublishing.com

Consultants: Dominique A. Didier, PhD, Associate Professor, Department of Biology, Millersville University;
Marla Conn, ReadAbility, Inc.
Book design: Sleeping Bear Press

Photo Credits: ©Christian Musat/Shutterstock Images, cover, 1, 12; ©Purestock/Thinkstock, 5; ©Rich Carey/
Shutterstock Images, 6; ©Four Oaks/Shutterstock Images, 7; ©Hiroshi Sato/Shutterstock Images, 9; ©Dorling
Kindersley RF/Thinkstock, 10; © iStockphoto/Thinkstock, 11, 21, 23; ©FannyOldfield/iStockphoto, 15; ©jo Crebbin/
Shutterstock Images, 17; ©VladGaviloff/Shutterstock Images, 18; ©Michael Rothschild/Shutterstock Images, 25;
©sturti/iStockphoto, 27; ©Mike Price/Shutterstock Images, 28; ©Willyam Bradberry/Shutterstock Images, 29

Library of Congress Cataloging-in-Publication Data

Thomas, Elizabeth, 1953- author.
Bottlenose dolphins / Elizabeth Thomas.
   pages cm. — (Exploring our oceans)
  Summary: "Introduces facts about bottlenose dolphins, including physical features, habitat, life cycle, food,
  and threats to these ocean creatures. Photos, captions, and keywords supplement the narrative of this
  informational text"— Provided by publisher.
  Audience: 8-12.
  Audience: Grades 4 to 6.
  Includes bibliographical references and index.
  ISBN 978-1-62431-598-5 (hardcover) — ISBN 978-1-62431-610-4 (pbk) —
  ISBN 978-1-62431-622-7 (pdf) — ISBN 978-1-62431-634-0 (ebook)
  1. Bottlenose dolphin—Juvenile literature. I. Title.

  QL737.C432T47 2014
  599.53'3—dc23   2013040970

Cherry Lake Publishing would like to acknowledge the work of
The Partnership for 21st Century Skills. Please visit www.p21.org
for more information.

Printed in the United States of America
Corporate Graphics Inc.
January 2014

ABOUT THE AUTHOR

Elizabeth Thomas is the author of several books for children. She received her master of fine arts
degree in Writing for Children and Young Adults from Hamline University in St. Paul, Minnesota.
She lives on Cape Cod, Massachusetts.

TABLE OF CONTENTS

CHAPTER 1

A BELOVED ANIMAL

Bottlenose dolphins have been much-loved creatures since ancient times. They have been written about in myths and folktales for centuries. In modern times, these marine **mammals** have been the stars of movies and television shows. They appear to do playful tricks as they leap out of the water. They are naturally curious about humans and are very intelligent. Their curving mouths seem to be grinning at everything they see. These dolphins have even been credited with saving the lives of people who were in danger of drowning.

Dolphins are mammals and come to the water's surface for air.

If a dolphin is injured, other dolphins will come to help it.

Dolphins live all over the world in the **temperate** and tropical waters of the Atlantic and Pacific Oceans. They typically do not live in cold waters. Some groups live closer to the shore and make visits into bays and lagoons. Others live farther out to sea, and some can live as far out as the edge of the **continental shelf**.

They are social animals and typically live in groups of between 15 and 30. At times, groups of bottlenose dolphins will join together in one group that numbers in the hundreds!

Some scientists think dolphins jump while traveling because jumping requires less energy than swimming through the water.

LOOK AGAIN

LOOK AT THIS PHOTOGRAPH CLOSELY. WHAT CAN YOU LEARN ABOUT THE BOTTLENOSE DOLPHIN FROM THIS PHOTO THAT YOU HAVEN'T LEARNED FROM THE CHAPTER?

CHAPTER 2

SLEEK SWIMMERS

Bottlenose dolphins vary in size, depending on where they live. The largest bottlenose dolphins have been found living in the chilly, dark waters around the British Isles. Larger dolphins have an easier time staying warm, so they are able to dive deeply in the cooler water. There, the males can grow to be almost 13 feet (4 m) long and weigh close to 1,400 pounds (635 kg). In warm waters they are much smaller. The males there are nearly 8.5 feet (2.6 m) long and weigh 660 pounds (299 kg). In all cases the females are slightly smaller than the males.

Dolphins are perfectly designed for swimming.

BODY DIAGRAM

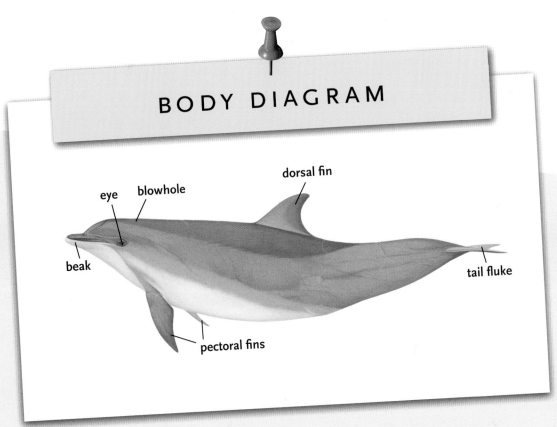

A dolphin's nose is also called a beak.

Dolphins have sleek, rocket-shaped bodies that allow them to skim through the water quickly. Their long, narrow, flexible skeleton also makes them excellent swimmers. Usually they swim at about 3 to 7 miles per hour (5 to 11 kph), but they can swim in bursts of up to 18 to 22 mph (29 to 35 kph). The dorsal fin, on the back

Dolphins have coloring similar to that of some sharks.

of their body, helps them swim in a straight line. Their rounded head and pointed snout also help them glide easily through the water.

The top of their body is dark gray. Their underside is usually a lighter gray, white, or pinkish gray. This coloring, called **countershading**, helps dolphins hide from predators. When seen from above, the darker color blends in with the water. When seen from below, the lighter color blends in with the sunlit surface of the sea.

If a dolphin loses a tooth, a new one does not grow in to replace it.

Bottlenose dolphins get their name from their nose shape. To some people, this shape looks like a bottle. The nose is about 3 inches (7.6 cm) long. Their mouth has up to 108 sharp, cone-shaped teeth. The teeth are designed for holding, not chewing, food. In the front of their head is a large, round forehead called a melon.

The bottlenose dolphin has very good hearing. Ear holes are on each side of its head near the corners of its mouth. Dolphins communicate using an assortment of noises including clicks, whistles, and chirps. Each dolphin has a special whistle. If a dolphin ever finds itself in trouble, it uses this whistle to call for help from the rest of the **pod**.

Dolphins also have excellent vision. Because their eyes are located on either side of their head, they have full 360-degree vision. They can see well both in the water and when their head is out of the water.

All mammals, including dolphins, have lungs. Dolphins must come to the surface to breathe air. At the top of a dolphin's head is a blowhole. This is the dolphin's one nostril. It is covered by a muscular flap that keeps water out. Dolphins use their blowhole to breathe and also to make noises to communicate.

THINK ABOUT IT

READ THIS CHAPTER CLOSELY. WHAT IS ONE OF ITS MAIN IDEAS? PROVIDE TWO POINTS FROM THE TEXT THAT SUPPORT THIS.

— CHAPTER 3 —

CRAFTY HUNTERS

Bottlenose dolphins are **carnivores**. Depending on where they live, they will eat small fish, squid, shrimp, crabs, and other sea creatures. Eels, octopus, and lobster are also part of a dolphin's diet. It is estimated that an active, male dolphin needs to eat 15 to 30 pounds (7 to 14 kg) of food every day.

Dolphins have several different ways to catch their prey. Since they have good eyesight both above and beneath the water, they can find prey with their eyes.

14

[21ST CENTURY SKILLS LIBRARY]

Dolphins in captivity eat fish fed to them by trainers.

In dark or deep water, they use **echolocation** to locate prey. The dolphin can learn the size, speed, direction, and distance of prey using echolocation. To do this dolphins send a sound wave that is transmitted through the melon in their head. The sound wave will bounce off of objects in front of the dolphin. The dolphin can detect these bounced sound waves and can use this information to navigate and to catch its prey.

Dolphins also use their snouts like shovels and dig in the sand at the bottom of the ocean for fish. This technique is called bottom grubbing. Another method dolphins use to capture prey is called fish whacking. Fish are smacked into shallow waters close to shore by a dolphin's powerful **flukes**. The stunned fish are then easy for the dolphin to eat.

Sometimes dolphins hunt together as a pod. They swim in a circle around a school of fish and drive them to a smaller space. Then other dolphins will swim through and eat from the school of fish.

Dolphins are social animals and often travel in a group.

A dolphin's eyes are on the side of its head, in line with the jaw hinge.

Their teeth are not designed for chewing, so they swallow their food whole. To avoid getting hurt by fins or tail spines, they usually eat prey headfirst. If they catch a fish that is too big to swallow whole, they will beat it against the ocean floor until it breaks into smaller pieces.

GO DEEPER

WHAT IS IT ABOUT THE PREY'S BODY THAT REQUIRES A DOLPHIN TO EAT IT HEADFIRST?

CHAPTER 4

MOTHERS AND BABIES

When a female bottlenose dolphin is between 5 and 13 years old, she will find a mate and start having babies. The babies are called calves. Dolphins can have calves every two to three years. They are pregnant for about 12 months. When it is time to give birth, the mother dolphin will go away from the pod and move close to the water's surface. Sometimes another dolphin will be on hand to help. Usually, only one baby is born.

Dolphin calves are born tail first in the water. Newborns are about 3 feet long (1 m) and weigh 22 to 44 pounds (10 to 20 kg). They are born knowing how to swim and need to get to the surface for their first breath of air. They can sometimes do this by themselves. Often the mother or a helper will assist the newborn in getting to the water's surface. Newborns stay near their mothers for protection.

A mother dolphin protects her baby. They stay together for several years.

The calves nurse until they are about 18 months old. But they can start catching and eating small fish at about six months of age. They do this by swimming belly-up and trapping fish very near the surface of the water. This method of hunting is called snacking.

Even after they stop nursing, mothers and calves stay very close to each other for up to six years. Mothers teach their young about finding food, avoiding predators, and communicating. One of the first things a mother dolphin does is repeat her unique whistle for her calf over and over. This helps the calf find her if they ever get separated.

Female bottlenose dolphins in the wild can live for almost 50 years. The males do not live quite as long.

Baby dolphins don't need to be taught how to swim.

LOOK AGAIN

LOOK CLOSELY AT THIS PHOTOGRAPH. WHAT IS THE
MOTHER DOLPHIN DOING TO HELP HER CALF?

THREATS AND PREDATORS

Any animal living in the wild has to learn to avoid danger. Dolphins do, too. Sometimes they are killed and eaten by other animals. These include tiger sharks, dusky sharks, and bull sharks. Killer whales have been known to kill dolphins, too, but this is very rare. Bottlenose dolphins have been known to attack and even kill sharks. Large male dolphins sometimes swim out in front of the pods and offer protection from predators.

Infections, stomach ulcers, heart disease, tumors, and breathing problems cause dolphins to become ill and die. They can also get **parasites** like tapeworms or roundworms.

This tiger shark and other sharks are predators of bottlenose dolphins.

Unfortunately, the biggest threats to these dolphins come from humans. In the past, dolphins were hunted for their fat and their skin. While this hunting has mostly stopped, dolphins still get caught in fishing nets that are meant to catch other types of sea creatures.

In some countries, nets are put in the water near swimming beaches to keep out sharks. But dolphins have died after getting tangled in those nets. Motorized boats are another threat. Dolphins can be injured by the propellers. Also, heavy boat traffic is noisy. It may interfere with the dolphin's echolocation as well as with its ability to communicate with other dolphins.

Pollution is also a threat to dolphins. Ocean currents carry polluted materials hundreds of miles out to sea. Sewage and the effects of oil spills are not healthy for dolphins.

Bottlenose dolphins are not considered **endangered**. All marine mammals, including dolphins, are protected by the U.S. Marine Mammal Protection Act of 1972.

Researchers investigate the death of this dolphin, washed up on shore near a pipeline.

Dolphins seem pleased to show off during aquarium shows.

Bottlenose dolphins are friendly, curious about people, and smart. They can be taught to perform tricks and entertain audiences. They are also of great interest to scientists who want to learn more about them. Dolphins live in aquariums all around the world. Aquariums allow scientists to more easily observe their day-to-day activities. But some people think it is cruel to keep such smart animals in captivity. Although bottlenose dolphins can survive well in captivity, calves born in captivity have less chance of surviving than calves born in the wild.

Many people care about bottlenose dolphins and are working hard to keep them safe and healthy.

Divers are able to swim near bottlenose dolphins without much fear of being hurt.

LOOK AGAIN

WHAT MIGHT SWIMMERS IN THIS PHOTOGRAPH BE THINKING? WOULD THEY FEEL THREATENED OR SAFE THAT CLOSE TO A BOTTLENOSE DOLPHIN?

THINK ABOUT IT

- What was the most surprising fact you learned about bottlenose dolphins from reading this book? Is there anything else you would like to know?

- Visit the library and check out another book about the bottlenose dolphin. How does the information in that book compare to the information in this one?

- Echolocation is an important skill that bottlenose dolphins use to catch prey. Humans can't echolocate, but we can mimic the way in which a dolphin produces sound. Try this: close your mouth, hold your nose, and cover your ears, then hum. What other animals use echolocation?

LEARN MORE

FURTHER READING

Miller-Schroeder, Patricia. *Bottlenose Dolphins*. Austin, TX: Raintree Steck-Vaughn Publishers, 2002.

Prevost, John F. *Bottlenose Dolphins*. Edina, MN: Abdo & Daughters, 1995.

Reeves, Randall R., Brent S. Stewart, Phillip J. Clapham, and James A. Powell. *National Audubon Society Guide to Marine Mammals of the World*. New York: Alfred A. Knopf, 2002.

Samuels, Amy. *Follow That Fin! Studying Dolphin Behavior*. Austin, TX: Raintree Steck-Vaughn, 2000.

Thompson, Paul, and Ben Wilson. *Bottlenose Dolphins*. Stillwater, MN: Voyageur Press, 1994.

WEB SITES

MarineBio
www.marinebio.org
This Web site is dedicated to sharing the wonders of the ocean and promoting science education.

National Geographic Kids—Bottlenose Dolphins
http://kids.nationalgeographic.com/kids/animals/creaturefeature/bottlenose-dolphin
Find lots of information and a video about dolphins.

SeaWorld—Bottlenose Dolphins
www.seaworld.org/animal-info/info-books/bottlenose
Learn about the dolphins' habitat, behavior, eating habits, and much more on this Web site.

GLOSSARY

carnivores (KAHR-nuh-vorz) animals that eat other animals

continental shelf (kahn-tuh-NEN-tuhl SHELF) the area of the seafloor near a coastline

countershading (KOUN-tur-shay-ding) the light and dark coloring of an animal to help it blend into its surroundings

echolocation (eh-koh-loh-KAY-shun) a process for locating a distant object by detecting sound waves reflected back from that object

endangered (en-DAYN-jurd) at risk of becoming extinct or of dying out

flukes (FLOOKS) flattened tail portions of a dolphin or whale

mammals (MAM-uhlz) warm-blooded animals that breathe air, give birth to live young, and feed them with milk

parasites (PAR-uh-sites) animals or plants that live on or inside of another animal or plant

pod (PAHD) small group of marine animals

temperate (TEM-pur-it) mild temperatures

INDEX

[21ST CENTURY SKILLS LIBRARY]